Baseball GOATs

The Greatest Athletes of All Time

BY BRUCE BERGLUND

CAPSTONE PRESS
a capstone imprint

Published by Capstone Press, an imprint of Capstone
1710 Roe Crest Drive, North Mankato, Minnesota 56003
capstonepub.com

Library of Congress Cataloging-in-Publication Data
Names: Berglund, Bruce R., author. Title: Baseball GOATs : the greatest athletes of all time / by Bruce Berglund. Other titles: Baseball greatest of all time
Description: North Mankato, Minnesota : Capstone Press, [2022] | Series: Sports illustrated kids: goats | Includes bibliographical references and index. | Audience: Ages 8-11 | Audience: Grades 4-6 | Summary: "How do you pick baseball's GOATs? Is Sandy Koufax the greatest pitcher to take the mound? Is Ted Williams the greatest pure hitter the game has seen? It comes down to stats, history, and hunches. Read more about some of the legends of baseball and see if you agree that they're the greatest of all time"—Provided by publisher
Identifiers: LCCN 2021042152 (print) | LCCN 2021042153 (ebook) | ISBN 9781663975478 (hardcover) | ISBN 9781666321487 (paperback) | ISBN 9781666321494 (pdf) | ISBN 9781666321517 (kindle edition)
Subjects: LCSH: Baseball players—Juvenile literature. | Pitchers (Baseball)—Juvenile literature. | Baseball—Records—Juvenile literature.
Classification: LCC GV867.5 .B46 2022 (print) | LCC GV867.5 (ebook) | DDC 796.357092/2—dc23
LC record available at https://lccn.loc.gov/2021042152
LC ebook record available at https://lccn.loc.gov/2021042153

Editorial Credits
Editor: Kristen Mohn; Designer: Sarah Bennett; Media Researcher: Svetlana Zhurkin; Production Specialist: Katy LaVigne

Image Credits
Alamy: Everett Collection Historical, 19; Associated Press: 15, Matty Zimmerman, 12, RHH, 25; Getty Images: Sporting News, 13; Library of Congress: cover (bottom left), 4, 17, 29; Newscom: Icon SMI/Sporting News Archives, 21 (top); Shutterstock: Apostle (star background), cover, back cover, 1, 30–31, 32, Keeton Gale, 5, Michal Sanca, 21 (bottom), Sunward Art (star confetti), 4, 6, 12, 18, 24; Sports Illustrated: Damian Strohmeyer, 11, Hy Peskin, 8, John G. Zimmerman, cover (top left), John Iacono, cover (bottom right), 22, John W. McDonough, cover (top middle), 16, Richard Meek, 6, 24, Robert Beck, cover (top right and bottom middle), 10, 26, 27, Walter Iooss Jr., 9

All records and statistics in this book are current through the 2020 season.

Printed and bound in China. 6667

Table of Contents

Words in **bold** appear in the glossary.

How to Pick Baseball's Greatest?

Baseball is an old sport. For as long as the game has been played, fans have **debated** who is the GOAT—the greatest player of all time.

It's hard to choose one player. Do you pick a great hitter or a great pitcher? Do you choose a player who broke records or a player who was among the best in Major League Baseball (MLB) year after year? Or do you choose someone who won the World Series several times?

Cy Young won 511 games as a pitcher—the all-time record. But during his career, pitchers played many more games in a season than they do today.

Clayton Kershaw is one of the modern era's best pitchers. He will never get close to 511 wins, but Kershaw gives up fewer hits and strikes out more batters than Cy Young did.

Because baseball is so old, the game has changed a lot. How do we compare players from the 1800s to players from the 1920s to players of today?

It's fun to debate the greatest players. After reading this book, you can make your own list of the greatest baseball players ever. Then ask other baseball fans what they think. Everyone has their own idea of who deserves the title GOAT.

Greatest Hitters

Hank Aaron

How do we pick the greatest hitter? Is it the player with the most total hits? Is it the player with the most home runs? Or is it the player who got the most RBIs (runs batted in)?

There is only one player in the top three of each of those MLB hitting records—hits, home runs, and RBIs. Hank Aaron could do it all when he stepped up to the plate.

Aaron was one of the most **consistent** batters ever. He hit at least 20 home runs for 20 seasons in a row. No other MLB player has done that.

Aaron at bat for the Milwaukee Braves during the 1957 World Series

Big Hitters

Most Hits in MLB History

Hitter	Years Played	Teams	Hits
Pete Rose	1963–1986	Reds, Phillies, Expos	4,256
Ty Cobb	1905–1928	Tigers, Athletics	4,189
Hank Aaron	1954–1976	Braves, Brewers	3,771

Most Home Runs

Hitter	Years Played	Teams	Home Runs
Barry Bonds	1986–2007	Pirates, Giants	762
Hank Aaron	1954–1976	Braves, Brewers	755
Babe Ruth	1914–1935	Red Sox, Yankees, Braves	714

Most Runs Batted In

Hitter	Years Played	Teams	Runs Batted In
Hank Aaron	1954–1976	Braves, Brewers	2,297
Albert Pujols	2001–2022	Cardinals, Angels	2,218
Babe Ruth	1914–1935	Red Sox, Yankees, Braves	2,213

Ted Williams

When baseball fans debate the greatest players, they sometimes talk about players with the best skills. Fans often say that the most skilled hitter was Ted Williams. Some even say his swing was perfect.

In 1942, Williams led MLB in batting average, home runs, and RBIs. After the season, he joined the military and fought in World War II.

Williams was a consistent hitter who could get on base with a single or double. He is the last MLB hitter to have a season batting average over .400. In some seasons he had an on-base percentage above .500. This means he got on base with a hit or walk more than half of the times he came to the plate. That is amazing!

Williams was also a power hitter. In the 1941 season, he batted over .400 and led the major leagues with 37 home runs. Williams even hit a home run in the last at bat of his career.

Since Williams batted .406 in 1941, no MLB player has reached the .400 mark. Tony Gwynn came closest when he batted .394 in 1994.

Ichiro Suzuki

Hank Aaron and Ted Williams started playing MLB when they were 20 years old. Ichiro Suzuki started with the Mariners when he was 27 years old. He had already played nine seasons of pro baseball in his home country of Japan.

Suzuki was a superstar right away in MLB. He led the league in batting average in 2001. He won the Rookie of the Year and the Most Valuable Player (MVP) awards in the same season.

Three years later, Suzuki broke the record for most hits in a season, with 262. The old record of 257 hits had lasted 84 years.

Suzuki got more than 200 hits per season for 10 years in a row. He is the only MLB player to do that.

When we add all of the hits Suzuki got in his 19 years in MLB together with all the hits he got in Japan, his total is 4,367 hits—the most for any pro baseball player.

Award Winners

Fourteen players have won two of baseball's major awards in the same season. In the 2000s, only three players have done this.

Player	Team	Year	Most Valuable Player	Cy Young Award	Rookie of the Year
Ichiro Suzuki	Mariners	2001	✔		✔
Justin Verlander	Tigers	2011	✔	✔	
Clayton Kershaw	Dodgers	2014	✔	✔	

Justin Verlander

Greatest Pitchers

Satchel Paige

Before 1947, Black players were not allowed on MLB teams. Instead, they played pro baseball in the Negro Leagues. During the winter, many players from the Negro Leagues and from MLB played each other in **exhibition** games. Everyone agreed that the best pitcher of all was from the Negro Leagues. His name was Satchel Paige.

Paige warms up before pitching for the Kansas City Monarchs in a game against the New York Cuban Stars.

Black players started playing on MLB teams after Jackie Robinson integrated MLB and joined the Dodgers in 1947. Before that, Robinson (right) and Paige (middle) were teammates in the Negro Leagues.

After playing 18 seasons in the Negro Leagues, Paige started playing in MLB in 1948. He was 42 years old—an age when most players **retire**. Fans packed into stadiums to see the famous pitcher.

Paige pitched in MLB again when he was 59 years old. Three years later, he pitched in an exhibition game against Hank Aaron. Aaron was 25 years younger. Paige threw two strikes and then got Aaron out on a weak pop-up. He was as old as a grandpa, but he could still beat the best hitter in baseball.

Sandy Koufax

Satchel Paige played baseball for a long time. Sandy Koufax played for a short time. In Koufax's 12 seasons with the Dodgers, he was the best pitcher in the league.

Koufax had a blazing fastball and a curveball that left hitters swinging at air. "Hitting against Sandy Koufax is like trying to eat soup with a fork," said one batter. In 1965, Koufax beat a 60-year-old record for most strikeouts in a season with 382. His career four no-hitters also set a record.

ERA Record

Baseball has many **statistics**. For pitchers, an important statistic is earned run average (ERA). This statistic says how many runs a pitcher gives up over a nine-inning game. An ERA under 4.00 is good. An ERA under 3.00 is great. An ERA under 2.00 is amazing.

Koufax led the league in ERA for five years in a row. In three of those seasons, his ERA was less than 2.00.

Because Koufax retired so early in his career, he was elected to the Baseball Hall of Fame when he was only 36 years old—the youngest player ever.

Koufax dominated hitters, but he was in terrible pain. He had a medical condition called arthritis that affected his pitching arm. Nothing doctors tried could stop the pain. After leading the league in wins, strikeouts, and **shutouts** in 1966, Koufax stopped playing. Even with a short career, Koufax is still one of baseball's best pitchers.

Randy Johnson

Randy Johnson was one of the tallest players in MLB history. He was 6 feet, 10 inches tall. That's taller than LeBron James. Just like James overpowers players on the basketball court, Johnson overpowered hitters on the baseball field.

Johnson won the Cy Young Award five times, including four years in a row.

Johnson was a flamethrower—a pitcher who throws hard fastballs and strikes out a lot of batters. He led the league in strikeouts nine times in his career.

Fast pitchers can be wild. At first, Johnson was wild. He gave up a lot of walks, and he hit a lot of batters. But then he worked on his ability to control his pitches. That's when he became a **dominant** pitcher.

Walter Johnson was baseball's first great power pitcher. He led the league in strikeouts for eight straight seasons in the 1910s. He has the all-time record for shutouts with 110. Randy Johnson had only 37 shutouts in his career.

Greatest Champions

Joe DiMaggio

Some players are all-time greats because they set records, like Sandy Koufax. Some are all-time greats because they were among the best players year after year, like Hank Aaron. Some are all-time greats because they had amazing skills, like Satchel Paige.

Others are all-time greats because they led their teams to championships.

The team with the most World Series wins is the Yankees, with 27 titles. The Yankees had many great players on their winning teams. The Yankee who stands out as the team's greatest is Joe DiMaggio.

In DiMaggio's 13 seasons with the Yankees, the team won the World Series nine times. DiMaggio was the team's best player. He was an All-Star every season he played, and he won the MVP award three times.

In 1941, DiMaggio got a hit in 56 straight games. Some people say this is baseball's greatest record—one they predict will never be broken.

Lords of the Rings

When a team wins a championship, each player gets a ring. Because the Yankees have won the most championships, famous Yankee players have a lot of rings.

Yankee Player	Years Played	Number of Rings
Yogi Berra	1946–1963	10
Joe DiMaggio	1936–1942, 1946–1951	9
Lou Gehrig	1923–1939	8
Mickey Mantle	1951–1968	7
Derek Jeter	1995–2014	5

Bob Gibson

Bob Gibson won only two championships. But he is one of the greatest World Series players ever.

Gibson's Cardinals faced the Yankees in the 1964 World Series. Each team won three games, and it came down to game seven. Gibson pitched all nine innings—a complete game—and the Cardinals won. In his three games pitching, Gibson struck out 31 Yankees—a World Series record. He was named the World Series MVP that year.

Gibson was even better in 1967 against the Red Sox. Again, the Cardinals won in seven games. Gibson pitched three complete games. He gave up only three runs and won all three games. Once again, he was World Series MVP.

The Cardinals were back the next year. Gibson struck out a record 17 batters in game one. Even though he pitched in game seven, the Cardinals lost a close one to the Tigers. Gibson missed his third ring, but he is remembered as one of the greatest World Series pitchers.

Gibson had one of the greatest seasons ever for a pitcher in 1968. His success was part of the reason MLB changed the height of the pitcher's mound from 15 inches to 10 inches to increase hits.

Changing the Strike Zone

Gibson and other pitchers performed so well in 1968 that MLB made the strike zone smaller. But the next year Gibson achieved even more strikeouts with the smaller strike zone.

MLB strike zone in 1968

MLB strike zone in 1969

Reggie Jackson

Reggie Jackson was an amazing athlete. He went to college to play football. One day after practice, he went to the baseball field to ask if he could join the team. The coach told him to try hitting. Jackson was still wearing his football uniform, but he hit a home run off the first pitch.

Jackson played his best in the month of October, when the World Series is usually held. He earned the nickname "Mr. October."

Jackson led the league in home runs four times. He hit more than 20 homers in a season 16 times. When he played, he was the most famous slugger in baseball.

Jackson was even better in the playoffs. He was World Series MVP twice. He won three straight rings with the Athletics and then two more after joining the Yankees. In his first World Series with the Yankees, he hit a record five home runs—including three in the final game.

World Series MVPs

Only four players have been named World Series MVP twice.

PLAYER	TEAM(S)	YEARS
Sandy Koufax	Dodgers	1963, 1965
Bob Gibson	Cardinals	1964, 1967
Reggie Jackson	Athletics, Yankees	1973, 1977
Corey Seager	Dodgers, Rangers	2020, 2023

Greatest All-Around Players

Willie Mays

Baseball has great hitters, great pitchers, and great champions. A few are all-time greats because they **excelled** in several parts of the game. They could get hits and walks, steal bases, drive in runs, blast homers, and stop the other team from scoring with amazing fielding.

Willie Mays played in 24 All-Star Games. He has the record for most total hits with 23 and runs with 20 in the All-Star Game.

When baseball fans talk about the greatest all-around players, the name that always comes up is Willie Mays. During his long career, Mays was near the top of all offensive categories. Season after season, he was in the top ten for batting average, homers, doubles, runs, and RBIs.

Above all, Mays was known for playing center field. Mays made one of the greatest defensive plays in baseball history during the 1954 World Series. With the score tied in the eighth inning, a batter hit a fly ball over Mays's head. Mays ran straight back toward the fence, caught the ball over his shoulder, and quickly threw the ball back to the infield. The Giants won the game and the series. Baseball fans call the play "The Catch."

Clemente's Golden Glove

Willie Mays and Hank Aaron played outfield at the same time. But some say another player at the time was an even better fielder. Roberto Clemente won 12 Gold Glove awards as a right fielder—as many as Mays won in center field.

Clemente had the strongest arm of any outfielder. Mays threw out 195 base runners from the outfield. Clemente threw out 266 runners!

Mike Trout

Mike Trout has played 14 seasons, and he's still playing. Can we already call him one of the greatest of all time? The answer is yes.

From his first season, baseball experts predicted that Trout would be one of the best players in MLB. He was named Rookie of Year and came in second for MVP. Since then, he has won the MVP award three times.

Trout bats for the Los Angeles Angels in a game against the Houston Astros.

Now, baseball experts say Trout is one of the best ever. These experts compare Trout's statistics in his first seasons to statistics of the all-time greats in their first seasons. In some hitting categories, Trout is ahead of Hank Aaron, Ted Williams, and Willie Mays.

Maybe if his career lasts 20 or more seasons, like other all-time greats, Trout will end up setting baseball's greatest records.

Trout is also an outstanding center fielder. In his first 10 seasons, he made only 20 errors on fielding plays. By comparison, Willie Mays made 74 errors in his first 10 seasons.

The First 1,000 Games

How has Trout done in his first 1,000 games compared to baseball's greatest in their first 1,000 games?

Home Runs	Doubles	On-Base Percentage
Mike Trout, 224	Mike Trout, 216	Mike Trout, .414
Ted Williams, 220	Willie Mays, 185	Joe DiMaggio, .402
Hank Aaron, 211	Roberto Clemente, 176	Willie Mays, .390

Babe Ruth

Only one player in baseball history was one of the best pitchers in MLB and then became the game's greatest hitter.

Only one player changed the way all teams try to score runs. Baseball offense used to be based on hitting singles and stealing bases. After this player, teams started using extra-base hits and homers to score runs.

Only one baseball player was a superstar outside of baseball. He appeared in movies and on the radio. His picture was always in magazines and ads.

Only one baseball player was a superstar around the world.

That player was Babe Ruth. His career began more than 100 years ago. But he is still the most famous player in baseball history—and the greatest of all time.

Ruth at bat in the early 1920s

The Greatest Season Ever

In 1921, Ruth set records for home runs, RBIs, runs scored, extra-base hits, slugging percentage, and total bases. Some of those records were later broken, even by Ruth himself. But that record-setting season is still the greatest ever by a hitter.

Ruth's 1921 Stats
.378 batting average
.512 on-base percentage
59 home runs
168 RBIs
177 runs

Glossary

consistent (kun-SISS-tent)—the same way, over and over, for a long time

debate (dih-BAYT)—to discuss a question, with arguments on both sides of the question

dominant (DAH-muh-nuhnt)—stronger than other players and able to control the game

excel (ek-SELL)—to be especially good at doing something

exhibition (ek-suh-BIH-shun)—games not played during the normal schedule and that do not count in the team's standings

retire (ree-TIRE)—to end a work career

shutout (SHUHT-out)—when a team does not score

statistics (stuh-TISS-tiks)—facts gathered in the form of numbers

Read More

Burrell, Dean. *Baseball Biographies for Kids: The Greatest Players from the 1960s to Today*. Emeryville, CA: Rockridge Press, 2020.

Frederick, Shane. *The World Series*. North Mankato, MN: Capstone, 2020.

Weakland, Mark. *Extreme Sports Records*. Mankato, MN: Black Rabbit Books, 2021.

Internet Sites

MLB
mlb.com

National Baseball Hall of Fame
baseballhall.org

Sports Illustated Kids: *"Baseball"*
sikids.com/baseball

Index

About the Author

photo by Marta Berglund

Bruce Berglund is a writer and historian. For 19 years, he taught history at Calvin College and the University of Kansas. His courses included the history of China, Russia, women in Europe, sports, and war in modern society. He has earned three Fulbright awards and traveled to 17 countries for research and teaching. His most recent book is *The Fastest Game in the World*, a history of world hockey published by the University of California Press. Bruce works as a writer at Gustavus Adolphus College, and he teaches writing classes at the Loft Literary Center in Minneapolis. His four children grew up reading books from Capstone Press, especially the graphic novel versions of classic literature. Bruce grew up in Duluth and now lives in southern Minnesota.